EXPOSING HIDDEN WORLDS

HOW JACOB RIIS' PHOTOS BECAME TOOLS FOR SOCIAL REFORM

by Michael Burgan

Content Adviser: Brett Barker, PhD
Associate Professor of History
University of Wisconsin–Marathon County

COMPASS POINT BOOKS
a capstone imprint

Compass Point Books are published by Capstone,
1710 Roe Crest Drive, North Mankato, Minnesota 56003
www.mycapstone.com

Editor: Catherine Neitge
Designers: Tracy Davies McCabe and Catherine Neitge
Media Researcher: Svetlana Zhurkin
Library Consultant: Kathleen Baxter
Production Specialist: Laura Manthe

Image Credits
Art Resource, N.Y.: The Museum of the City of New York, 39, 45; Bridgeman Images:
Museum of Fine Arts, Houston, Texas, USA/Gift of Howard Greenberg/*Waiting to Be
Let in the Mulberry Street Station, 1892* (gelatin silver print), Riis, Jacob August
(1849-1914), 47, Museum of the City of New York, USA/*Police Station Lodgers 19.
The Single typhus lodger in Eldridge Street, he lay by the stove in the policemen's
room no one dreaming what ailed him* (b/w photo), Riis, Jacob August (1849-1914),
49; Getty Images: Bettmann, 15, 24, 31, 56 (right), Corbis/Photo Collection
Alexander Alland Sr., 53, Museum of the City of New York/Jacob A. Riis, 9, 55, SSPL,
13, UIG/Universal History Archive, 50; Granger, NYC, cover, 32, 37, 58 (bottom);
Library of Congress, 17, 19, 23, 26, 35, 41, 43, 56 (left), 57, 58 (top), 59 (top);
Newscom: akg-images, 25, Picture History/Jacob A. Riis, 7, 11, 20, 29; Shutterstock:
Everett Historical, 5, 59 (bottom)

Library of Congress Cataloging-in-Publication Data

Cataloging-in-publication information is on file with the Library of Congress.
ISBN 978-0-7565-5618-1 (library binding)
ISBN 978-0-7565-5620-4 (paperback)
ISBN 978-0-7565-5622-8 (ebook pdf)

Printed in the United States of America
010374F17

TABLEOFCONTENTS

Chapter One

INTO THE SLUMS

Late on a fall night in 1887, journalist Jacob Riis headed out into the slums on the Lower East Side of New York City. Riis knew these dark streets and crowded buildings well. For 10 years, he had roamed the city looking for stories to write for the *New York Tribune* newspaper. He mostly wrote about police news, which included reporting on crimes, fires, and public health and safety. Riis wrote that he had covered "all the news that means trouble to some one."

Many of the people Riis saw and wrote about were immigrants. From 1881 to 1890, more than 5 million immigrants came to the United States. Many were poor and uneducated, and they struggled to find decent jobs. Large numbers came through the port of New York and then stayed there. By 1890 about 40 percent of the city's population had been born in another country.

Riis, too, was an immigrant. He was born and raised in Denmark. After coming to the United States, he had experienced bouts of poverty and knew what it was like to be homeless. As a reporter, he was determined to show other Americans what life was like in the slums of the country's largest city. Riis hoped that his reporting would lead the public and government officials to work together to improve

Jacob Riis' photo of an Italian immigrant mother and her baby appeared in his groundbreaking work that exposed the pain and suffering of New York City's poor.

living conditions for the people who were crowded together in run-down, dirty apartment buildings called tenements.

By the time Riis set out on that fall night in 1887, he had decided that words weren't enough. He wanted to show the brutal reality of the slums using images. Drawings wouldn't work. For one thing, as Riis readily admitted, he couldn't draw. And illustrations, he later wrote, "would not have been evidence of the kind I wanted." They would lack the realism and impact of photographs. Riis, who usually searched for stories at night, in buildings without electric lights, knew that the cameras available then couldn't take good pictures of what he wanted to show. Then he read about an invention that promised to change that.

Two German scientists had found that mixing three powdered chemicals and lighting them created a bright flash of light. Riis, along with amateur photographers in New York City, realized what this could mean for photography. Henry Piffard, one of the other New York photographers, tinkered with the mixture to make it safer to use. Then he put the chemicals in a cartridge and fired them from a gun. That method created a useful flash that was fairly safe. Piffard belonged to a photography club, along with Richard Hoe Lawrence and John Nagle. Riis knew Nagle, who worked in the city's Health Department. Riis asked him about using the new technology to photograph tenements at night. Nagle, Piffard, and Lawrence agreed to go with Riis on his first photographic missions.

Along with the three photographers and sometimes a police officer or two, Riis wrote, they set out, "bent on letting in the light where it was so much needed." He and his team often used what was called a detective camera, because it was smaller than most

Riis used a flash to illuminate the plight of a man who lived with three others in a filthy cellar. The man slept on a plank atop two barrels.

cameras of the day. The wooden box camera could be easily hidden or disguised so others wouldn't realize what it was. But Riis' team scared some tenement dwellers anyway, since they saw strange men enter their building with a flash gun. Riis explained that it was only for photography, but some people he encountered ran away. Sometimes the team burst into rooms and flashed their light before people inside knew what had happened. As art historian and photography scholar Bonnie Yochelson wrote, those pictures "retain their power today because the harsh light and haphazard compositions convey the chaos of living in poverty."

Riis hoped to use the pictures to produce what was called a magic lantern show. He already had done shows with this early kind of slide projector for more than 10 years. The lantern projected the photo on a wall or curtain large enough for many people to see at once, and Riis explained the image.

While he was working on putting a show together, Riis and his team were drawing interest from other newspapers. In February 1888, two New York papers ran stories about Riis' work and printed woodcuts based on his photographs. At the time, few newspapers illustrated their stories. Those that did sometimes used pen drawings. The woodcut engravings were copies of the images Riis' team members had made with their cameras. The technology to allow newspapers to easily print vivid photographs was still years away.

Some of the best-known photographs associated with Riis were made during his early trips into the slums. One of the most famous of the first pictures is called *Bandit's Roost*. It shows an alley with that name off of Mulberry Street. The street formed one border of an area known as Mulberry Bend, one of the worst slums in the city. It was near the larger Five Points neighborhood, which had long been known for its poverty and crime. Riis knew Mulberry Bend well, because his office was on Mulberry Street and he often explored alleys like Bandit's Roost. Riis

Bandit's Roost, Riis' 1888 photo of a Lower East Side street gang, was taken at 59½ Mulberry Street in Manhattan. It was in one of the most dangerous neighborhoods in New York City.

said that during his 20 years of reporting on crime, the neighborhood had appeared in police reports every week, "generally in connection with a crime of violence, a murder or a stabbing." According to city records, only two dozen of the hundreds of tenements in the area were in decent condition.

In the *Bandit's Roost* photo, a tough-looking man stands in the foreground. On either side of the picture are walls of tenements, reflecting the crowded nature of the alley and others like it. Other neighborhood residents stand around or lean out of windows. None of them may have been criminals, despite the name of the picture and the alley. But the image shows people who seem unhappy with their surroundings—or perhaps with being photographed.

Riis' work was tied to his interest in improving the living conditions of people who could not afford decent housing. Nagle and the other photographers, however, simply wanted to show what the new flash technology could do for photographers. Using the negatives, the photographers could make prints. But the photographers grew tired of the late-night trips into the slums. Wanting to press on with his mission, Riis hired two professional photographers to go with him on his nightly adventures for a short time. Finally he decided to buy a camera and take pictures himself.

Riis first experimented with his new device in January 1888 on Hart Island, a strip of land in Long Island Sound off the coast of the Bronx. There the city of New York buried poor people, criminals, and unclaimed bodies that could not be identified. The graves were in what was called a "potter's field." At the time, the city buried about 4,000 people there every year. Looking over the potter's field, Riis saw an open trench waiting to be filled with simple wooden coffins. He took a picture, but he was disappointed with the resulting print. He thought the image was too dark. Later, though, when he projected it through his magic lantern, the darkness gave the image more emotional power than if there had been more light. Riis wrote that the darkness "added a gloom to the show more realistic than any the utmost art of professional skill might have attained."

While he was documenting life in the slums, Riis prepared his first public lecture, which he called "The Other Half, How It Lives and Dies in New York." The title was similar to a line from an 1845 report

Riis would end his lectures with a photo of gravediggers placing coffins in a common grave at a potter's field.

on health conditions among New York's poor. The author of that report wrote that it "has often been said that 'one half does not know how the other half lives.'" Other authors later repeated variations of the phrase.

In his lecture, Riis projected 100 magic lantern images and described each scene. Not all of the images came from Riis or his team. Some were taken from books and from the local police station, where officers hung the pictures of well-known criminals in what was called the "Rogue's Gallery." The images in the show included *Bandit's Roost,* a criminal gang sharing drinks, and a rooming house that charged pennies a night to sleep there. To show how the "other half" dies, Riis included pictures of a hospital and the potter's field.

Several newspapers had stories about Riis' first lecture. The *New York Herald* said the photos "embraced not only the ordinary home life of tenement house dwellers, but also showed vividly many scenes in which vice and brutality reigned rampant." The *New Jersey News* called the pictures "shocking." Riis began taking his photos to New York churches, hoping he could enlist them in the effort to clean up the slums. Some churches, however, turned him down. The photos' startling realism, which some viewers admired, was too upsetting to others.

MAGIC LANTERNS

Humans have told each other stories and created pictures for tens of thousands of years. The magic lantern let storytellers combine images with their tales, and they could easily take the illustrated stories from place to place.

The first magic lanterns were invented during the late 1600s. They used candlelight to project an image from a glass plate onto a wall. The light went through the lantern's glass lens, which the storyteller could focus to sharpen the image. Over time magic lanterns used more powerful light sources, so the images could be bigger and seen by more people. Some of the earliest images showed supernatural beings, such as ghosts and demons, which may have led to the "magic" in the device's name.

By the 1800s some people could afford to buy their own lanterns to use at home. But many people still came to see magic lantern shows, such as the ones Riis presented. He wanted his shows to inform others, but he knew people saw them as entertainment too. Middle-class Americans were curious to see how people different from them, such as poor immigrants, lived. Although the magic lantern lost popularity to the movies, some entertainers still put on magic lantern shows with old machines.

A magic lantern was an early form of a slide projector.

Riis carried on, finding places in nearby states where he could deliver his talk and show his pictures. But he wanted to reach a larger audience. He asked editors of several national magazines whether they wanted to print his pictures and the stories that went with them. Finally, one editor agreed to publish his work.

The December 1889 issue of *Scribner's Magazine*

carried an article by Riis called "How the Other Half Lives: Studies Among the Tenements." It was illustrated by woodcut engravings of his photos. Riis described life in Mulberry Bend and similar neighborhoods, focusing on the ethnic groups settling in the city. He told of children left to roam the streets, and families who turned their cramped rooms into "factories." Business owners hired them to make such things as cigars or clothing at home.

The newcomers were not bad people, Riis said. They were just struggling to find good jobs and decent places to live. Riis hoped to show others the harsh conditions the immigrants faced so they would take steps to improve them. With his work, Riis became the first "muckraker"—a journalist who exposes the muck (filth) of society—to try to bring change. The term was not first used until the early 1900s, years after "How the Other Half Lives" was published. But Riis' work helped pave the way for the muckrakers who followed him. A whole movement to improve conditions for the poor, workers, and immigrants had begun by the early 1900s. It was known as the Progressive Movement, and Riis played an important role in its rise.

Riis expanded the *Scribner*'s article into a book. *How the Other Half Lives: Studies Among the Tenements of New York* described the history of housing in New York City and the slow conversion

Riis hoped to show others the harsh conditions the immigrants faced so they would take steps to improve them.

In *How the Other Half Lives*, Riis wrote that brothers John, 10, (left) and Willie, 8, told police they "didn't live nowhere." Riis continued that they "never went to school, could neither read nor write. Their twelve-year-old sister kept house for the father, who turned the boys out to beg, or steal, or starve."

of fine older homes into crowded apartments. Cheap new homes were built near them. The resulting slums, he wrote, led to the spread of sickness and the rise of crime. Riis called for enforcing the laws that covered housing and for building new tenements with better living conditions.

How the Other Half Lives won Riis praise for trying to correct what he saw as a terrible social evil. He later won fame as a pioneering photojournalist, and his influence is still felt today.

ChapterTwo
FROM DENMARK TO AMERICA

As an immigrant in a new land, Jacob Riis faced
many challenges before he became famous for his
pictures and descriptions of tenement life. He was
born in the Danish village of Ribe on May 3, 1849.
The town, said to be the oldest in Scandinavia, was
settled by Vikings more than 1,000 years earlier.
Ribe had once been a thriving town, but over the
centuries it lost its importance. Jacob's parents,
Niels Edvard and Carolina, had settled there just
three years before Jacob was born. His father was a
schoolteacher, and even with this steady work, the
Riis family sometimes struggled to get by. But Jacob
and his brothers and sisters never went hungry. Their
mother, a faithful Christian, taught them to help
others when they could.

Jacob's father spoke several languages, and Jacob
learned English while he was still a boy. One of his
favorite authors was Charles Dickens, who often
wrote about the harsh lives of England's poor and
working-class people as the country industrialized.
Jacob also had an early experience with putting
together a newspaper. His father edited a local paper
for a time, and Jacob helped.

While living in Ribe, Jacob first saw what
he thought was a tenement. An old building the

townspeople called Rag Hall was near what had once been the moat of an impressive castle. As an adult, Jacob recalled the "darkness and human misery" of the building, especially when compared with the beautiful green fields around it. Jacob hated dirt and filth, and he tried to do something about the conditions in at least one part of Rag Hall. One Christmas, he received a coin as a present. He went to the tenement and told the father of a poor family that he could have the coin if he would clean up his children and their living quarters.

Jacob's father hoped his son would become a teacher like him, but Jacob chose a different path. When he was 16, he went to the Danish capital of Copenhagen to become a carpenter. He returned to Ribe four years later and proposed marriage to Elizabeth Giortz, his first and only love. She didn't feel the same attraction to him, though, and she said no (this time). The rejection played a large part in Riis' decision to move to America. He sailed for New York in 1870, not knowing what to expect.

Newcomers, he wrote after arriving, "knew no distinction of West and East. By rights there ought to have been buffaloes and … Indians charging up and down Broadway." He said people in Denmark would find that easier to believe "than that New York is paved, and lighted with electric lights." New York, though, was already a city of almost 1 million people, and Brooklyn, then a separate city, had about 400,000 people of its own.

Riis soon went to Pennsylvania, where he put his carpentry skills to work. Struggling to make money, he considered returning to Denmark. He sold most of his possessions to go back to New York. Instead

Years after leaving for the United States, Jacob Riis returned to Ribe, Denmark, to visit his parents. His 1893 photograph features his mother, Carolina (in doorway), his father, Niels Edvard Riis, and his wife, Elizabeth.

of leaving the United States, however, he wandered, looking for work and sometimes going hungry and sleeping outdoors. He spent time in New York's Five Points area. Filled with overcrowded tenements, Five Points stank from human and animal waste; the city did not have sewers or garbage collection at the time. One night Riis, in despair, considered killing himself, but he found the strength to live

despite his poverty. He spent the night in a police station. Stations were sometimes used as homeless shelters during the winter. They were not equipped to handle the homeless, however, and only had simple pieces of wood for beds.

> "I think that I must have a flair for journalism, at least I'm successful at everything I do. I have my own office and, all in all, life is great."

Riis began to wander again, going back to Pennsylvania for a time, then to northern New York state. He did various jobs, including cutting ice out of ponds and selling furniture and then irons. He did well until the U.S. economy crashed in 1873. Millions of people lost their jobs, and Riis once again struggled to find food and shelter.

Then Riis saw a businessman he knew. The man told him about a job opening as a reporter at the New York News Association. It produced stories for the city's newspapers. During his time in the United States, Riis had thought about becoming a journalist, and now he had the chance. The editor at the news association sent him on a test assignment, and then hired him for the job.

Riis had to work seven days a week for 13 or 14 hours a day. But with his pay, he could afford housing and food. The job also kept his mind off Elizabeth Giortz, whom he still loved. While working there, Riis first saw Mulberry Bend, the neighborhood he later documented in *How the Other Half Lives*.

Riis left New York City in 1874 to work for a newspaper in Brooklyn. After just two weeks on the job, he took over as the editor. "I think that I must have a flair for journalism," he wrote in his diary, "at least I'm successful at everything I do. I have my own office and, all in all, life is great."

Riis had not forgotten about Elizabeth, and that

Christmas, he learned that the Danish soldier she was supposed to marry had died. Riis thought he still had a chance to win her love. The way to do it, he figured, was to become a successful business owner. Early in 1875, he bought the paper he was working for. Riis worked hard and made money, and then wrote to Elizabeth to propose. This time she accepted. Early in 1876 Riis returned to Denmark to marry her. He had sold the newspaper back to its first owners and made a good profit, so he could afford to travel and then return with his bride to Brooklyn.

Back in Brooklyn, Riis began to make money with a magic lantern. A new chemical process created a brighter light than a candle, and Riis and a partner used the lantern to project ads outdoors for local businesses. Riis wrote that he had considered it "honest, decent work," and said his images were "real work[s] of art." He and his partner took the business on the road, traveling in 1877 to Elmira, New York. Riis saw there that the economic crisis of 1873 was still causing problems for some workers. Railroads had faced particularly tough times, so they cut wages, and many railroad workers went on strike. While Riis had sympathy for the poor, he did not support the strikers, especially when they turned to violence. Workers and business owners, he later wrote, "need to understand each other and their common interests to see the folly of quarreling."

Riis soon gave up his advertising business and

Riis (in left corner) with fellow journalists at the *New York Tribune* police office on Mulberry Street

went back to journalism. He got a job with the *New York Tribune*, one of the major newspapers in the city. After covering various kinds of news for a few months, Riis in 1878 ended up in an office on Mulberry Street, where the *Tribune* kept its police reporter. The office was right across from police headquarters. Riis knew it was a hard assignment, but he was ready for the challenge.

During his years as a police reporter, Riis came to know something about life in the slums. He followed police officers and health inspectors into tenements,

Riis photographed a family living in a tenement in Poverty Gap, a block on Manhattan's West 28th Street.

where he saw families jammed into tiny, dark rooms. In the summer, extreme heat threatened to kill the elderly and infants, and horrible smells met him around every corner. Riis saw many children going hungry or turning to crime to stay alive. Riis wrote about the homeless in the streets and about a once-wealthy man who was spending his last days in a bare tenement room. He saw the bodies of people who had committed suicide and interviewed

Three women bundled up on the floor of a boardinghouse were the subject of Riis' camera.

relatives of people who had died in accidents. He later wrote that he and the other police reporters "did not gloat over the misfortunes we described. We were reporters, not ghouls." Not everyone liked Riis' writing style. At times he included his opinions rather than just reporting the facts. "But, good or bad," he said later, "I could write in no other way, and kept right on."

While New York City had always attracted

THE DAWN OF THE PROGRESSIVE ERA

A 1906 political cartoon featured journalists and politicians on a crusade against corruption.

Historians usually date the start of the Progressive Era to 1890—just as Jacob Riis' work was beginning to reach a wider audience.

Reformers reacted to the many changes brought about by America's rapid economic growth after the Civil War. Along with increased immigration, the country saw a boom in industry, which often led to harsh working conditions for employees. Another problem was corruption in city government—elected leaders used their positions to make money for themselves and their friends. Progressives wanted to end the corruption and have laws passed that would end the worst problems created by industrialization.

During the era, muckraking journalists such as Ida Tarbell, Lincoln Steffens, and Upton Sinclair documented the problems caused when companies faced little or no government limits on their actions.

immigrants, more of the people coming to the United States during the 1880s were from countries that had sent only a few immigrants in the past. For most of the country's history, large numbers of immigrants came from Great Britain, Ireland, Germany, and Scandinavia. The wave of so-called new immigrants now reaching the country came in large numbers from Italy, Greece, Eastern Europe, and Russia. Many were Jewish immigrants fleeing the discrimination they faced at home. The new arrivals stirred suspicion and fear. Some workers feared that the immigrants would take away jobs from Americans, or that companies would pay all workers less because the immigrants would work for lower wages.

Some nativists—people who wanted to restrict immigration by race and national origin—began to call for restrictions on immigration. *The Atlantic Monthly*, a national magazine, in 1892 published a poem, "Unguarded Gates," that described growing anti-immigrant feelings. A "wild motley throng" of people, the poem said, was passing through the country's "wide open and unguarded" gates, and speaking "strange tongues … accents of menace alien to our air."

As an immigrant himself, Riis did not share the nativists' fears. He believed most immigrants simply wanted to work hard and build a better life than the one they had left behind. But he did sometimes see the newcomers in stereotypical ways, and he shared his views in his reporting. In an 1883 article, he mentioned Jews who complained loudly about a tiny scratch and Italians who would refuse to tell police who had stabbed them in a fight. Instead, the victim would declare, "I fix him myself."

Riis also seemed to think immigrants should not keep their own culture but should become "Americanized." But in more recent times, some Americans saw that as insulting to immigrants. The attitude seemed to suggest that people could not keep their own culture and still be Americans.

With his views on immigrants, Riis biographer Tom Buk-Swienty wrote, Riis was like most native-born Americans and immigrants from northern Europe. They tended to look down on immigrants from southern and eastern Europe—particularly those immigrants who weren't Protestant. Yet in later writings Riis praised the traits he saw in many of the new immigrants. They were hardworking and honest. He also had kind words for the African-Americans in the slums and saw their loyalty to the United States, despite the history of slavery.

The new immigrants flooded into the tenements, and through the 1880s Riis wrote more stories about the conditions in the slums. He sometimes explored Bandit's Roost and other alleys that ran off

Riis noted in the caption of his photograph of a New York City slum that "it costs a dollar a month to sleep in these sheds."

of Mulberry Street. He was the first to call the area where the street turned "Mulberry Bend," and he came to know it well. He was very bothered by the dirty, overcrowded tenements that lined the alleys.

Other reformers also tried to improve life in the tenements. Riis covered the lectures of one of them, Felix Adler. He was the son of German Jewish immigrants who had come to New York during the 1850s. His family was well off, but he saw the difficulties poorer immigrants faced. Adler served on New York's Tenement House Commission, which investigated living conditions in the slums. The commission's 1884 report said life was getting worse in the tenements. It called for various reforms, such as providing plumbing, better lighting, and ventilation. Adler shared Riis' view that most of the urban poor were decent people. "It is not the squalid people that make the squalid houses," Adler said, "but the squalid houses that make the squalid people." Adler thought the worst tenements should be torn down and the state government should protect tenants from unfair landlords and promote public health.

Riis' decision to use photography to work for reform marked a turning point in his life. After buying his own camera, he struggled to master it. It was hard for him to use the flash at first, and once some of the lit powder went into his face. He later wrote, "Only my spectacles saved me from being blinded for life." But soon Riis was able to take good pictures. One of his most satisfying moments came when he helped prove that a Mulberry Bend landlord was breaking the law by crowding too many people into one tenement. Two rooms that should have held four or five people had 15 sleeping in them, without beds. When city officials turned in the report of their investigation, Riis' picture was with it. The photo showed the scene clearly, and the landlord could not claim that the report was wrong.

Riis' decision to use photography to work for reform marked a turning point in his life.

Riis' book featured a photograph of a Manhattan lodging house where more than a dozen people crowded into a small room. Space to sleep on the bare floor was available for 5 cents a night.

That incident showed Riis' approach to photography. For him, it was a tool to help right wrongs. He didn't care about the science behind cameras, but he loved what he called the "miracle" of watching an image appear on the glass plate. He wrote in his autobiography, "I am downright sorry to confess here that I am no good at all as a photographer for I would like to be."

With his photos and lectures, Riis started to spread the message of reform that was so important to him. His book *How the Other Half Lives* reached an even larger audience. The book was illustrated with the woodcuts that had been made for the *Scribner's* article, drawings, and reproductions of 15 of his photos. A new process for printing photos on paper, called halftone, made it easier to reproduce the photos. The pictures' quality was poor, but they still had an impact. Some of the photos, it was later revealed, were staged. He took two now-famous pictures of homeless newspaper boys whom he called "Street Arabs." Although the title of one photo says it was taken at night, Riis actually shot it in daylight. At times he paid boys to pose in his pictures. But while the shots were not really photojournalism because

Riis' famous photo, which he captioned *Street Arabs in Sleeping Quarters,* uses children as symbols of neglect by society.

they were staged, they showed a reality that Riis knew existed. He wrote that he had seen "little groups of these boys hanging about the newspaper offices; in winter, when snow is on the streets, fighting for warm spots around the grated vent-holes that let out the heat and steam from the underground press-rooms with their noise and clatter."

How the Other Half Lives included statistics about overcrowded housing in New York and the numbers of arrests for various crimes. One solution to the housing problem, Riis wrote, was to build model tenements and maybe give tax breaks to the investors who paid for them. He also called for arresting landlords who ignored the laws meant to protect tenants.

More than 80 newspapers carried reviews of the book, and most were positive. While one reviewer dismissed the artistic quality of the photos, another said "the pictures ... are true to life" and that Riis "is speaking of that which he knows and testifies of that which he has seen." Riis later wrote that he had been a little surprised by the book's success. "Perhaps it was that I had had it in me so long," he said, "that it burst out at last with a rush that caught on."

Riis, though, had not finished his crusade to rid New York City of its worst tenements. He wanted to tell the stories of more immigrants, with both pictures and words.

ChapterThree
THE OTHER HALF AND BEYOND

In his newspaper reporting and his book, Jacob Riis often wrote about the children of the tenements. In Denmark Riis had seen most of his brothers and sisters die shortly after birth or before they became adults. The cause was usually tuberculosis, a lung disease. But his brother Theodore drowned when he was just 9. Riis biographer Tom Buk-Swienty argued that seeing children's lives cut short deeply affected Riis. "It formed the basis of his conviction that, as a human race, the least we can do is to ensure our children a healthy upbringing."

Riis and Elizabeth raised their children in Queens, which was more rural than Brooklyn. There the children had fresh air and a backyard. Although still a hard worker, Riis tried to spend more time with his children. He sometimes told them about the bleak lives of tenement children.

In 1888, soon after Riis started his magic lantern show of *How the Other Half Lives*, his children developed scarlet fever. To cheer them up, Riis took a young flower outside and planted it. When the flower bloomed in the spring, the sick Riis children beamed, and they showed great pleasure as it continued to grow. In June, when they saw more flowers outside, the children asked their father to take flowers into the

Riis photographed his wife, Elizabeth (seated), and their children in 1898. It was most likely taken in their yard in Queens.

city when he visited the slums. They wanted the poor children there to experience the same joy they had felt because of a simple flower.

Riis set off one morning with a bunch of just-picked daisies to give to children in the slums. "I never got more than half a block from the ferry with my burden," he wrote in his autobiography. "The street children went wild over the 'posies.' They pleaded and fought to get near me, and when I had no flowers left to give them sat in the gutter and wept with grief. The sight of it went to my heart."

The incident drove Riis to write a letter to the *New York Tribune* asking others to do the same: bring fresh flowers into the city to give the urban poor a taste of natural beauty. Riis even offered to take flowers that people brought in and give them away himself. Soon, his office on Mulberry Street was filled with flowers, and children flocked there to get their own. The joy Riis saw as he gave out the flowers led him to write, "I had seen an armful of daisies keep the peace of a block better than the policeman's club."

But Riis knew that while flowers could brighten a life, they could not solve the problems of the tenements. He was particularly concerned about what the children there faced as they struggled to survive. In 1892 *Scribner's Magazine* published Riis' article "The Children of the Poor," which was illustrated with many of his photographs. Some are among his best known today. Several months later, he expanded the article into a book, just as he had done with *How the Other Half Lives*. "The two books are one," he wrote in the preface to *The Children of the Poor*. "Each supplements the other. Ours is an age of facts. It wants facts, not theories, and facts I have endeavored to set down in these pages." But along with the facts were the words and experiences of the children Riis had met in and around Mulberry Bend.

With his stories and pictures, Riis described children who had never experienced the kind of childhood most middle-class or wealthy children knew. One of them was Katie, a dark-haired girl of 9 who spent her days cooking and cleaning for her older sister and brothers. The children had gone off on their own after their mother had died and their father had remarried. Katie took care of their tenement room while her siblings worked. When she had time, she went to school, acquiring what Riis called "crumbs of learning."

Riis now often worked during the day rather than at night, as he had previously. Many of his subjects, including Katie, willingly posed for him. Her smileless face, though, reflects some of the hardness of her young life. When Riis asked her what kind of work she did, she simply answered, "I scrubs." Riis used

"I scrubs," said little Katie when Riis took a photo of her in 1891.

that statement as the caption for her photograph, and he noted that "her look guaranteed that what she scrubbed came out clean."

Riis also mentioned Pietro, a 13-year-old Italian boy he had met. Pietro had been hit by a streetcar and had spent months in a hospital. His severe injuries prevented him from starting work as a shoeshine boy, which he had planned. Now Pietro worked to improve his English language skills. A woodcut based on a Riis photo shows the boy hard at work at that task. *The Children of the Poor* had several of such woodcuts, as well as halftone pictures retouched by artists.

Another picture showed Susie, a young girl who worked during the day and went to school at night. Riis photographed her at her job, covering small pieces of tin with cloth. She worked so fast, Riis wrote, that even with the flash he could not clearly capture her hands. The photo shows just a blur of motion. Riis wrote about other children in Susie's neighborhood who earned money selling newspapers or artificial flowers they had made.

Not all the pictures in *The Children of the Poor* showed the youngest tenement residents. Riis explained that one showed where three peddlers "slept in the mouldy cellar, where the water was ankle deep on the mud floor. The feeblest ray of daylight never found its way down there. ... Sometimes the

water rose to the height of a foot, and never quite soaked away in the dryest season. It was an awful place."

Riis tried to show that the children of the poor had some hope. Many charities and other organizations were trying to educate them. He did not blame the children for their problems. It was the bad living conditions of the tenements, he argued, that shaped their lives. "The child is a creature of environment, of opportunity, as children are everywhere," he wrote. "The tough is not born: he is made. The all-important point is the one at which the manufacture can be stopped." Riis' solution was to "school the children first of all into good Americans, and next into useful citizens."

Riis once again won praise for his work, and some newspapers again pointed out the photos' power to vividly illustrate Riis' words. By the time the book came out, Riis had found an important ally in his efforts to reform New York's slums: Theodore Roosevelt, the future president of the United States.

A member of a wealthy New York family, Roosevelt had entered politics in his early 20s. He first served in the state legislature and then led a commission that tried to reform how U.S. government workers were hired. Even before Roosevelt became a nationally known politician, Riis thought Roosevelt could play an important role in achieving reform. After he read *How the Other Half Lives*, Roosevelt tried to visit Riis in his Mulberry Street office. Riis was out, so Roosevelt left a note: "I have read your book and I have come to help." Of the book, Roosevelt later wrote, "Jacob Riis had drawn an indictment of the things that were wrong, pitifully and dreadfully wrong, with the tenement homes and the tenement lives of our wage-workers. In his book he had pointed out how the city government, and especially those connected with the departments of police and health, could aid in remedying some of the wrongs."

CHILD LABOR

As he continued to deliver his illustrated lectures and write articles, Jacob Riis sometimes used pictures from other photographers, including Lewis Hine. Riis bought 11 of Hine's photos to illustrate one of his magazine articles.

Unlike Riis, Hine considered himself an artist as well as a reformer. Hine was also trained as a sociologist, someone who studies the social relationships between people and the institutions they create to make society work. Hine believed in the power of experts to document a problem and offer solutions for government to carry out. While Riis believed governments could make some positive changes, he thought good Christians like himself should give to charities as a way to solve many problems.

When Riis' career was nearing an end, Hine was traveling the country to document working conditions in factories and mines. He was particularly interested in showing the harsh conditions children faced in those places. At the time, the United States did not have strict laws against forcing children to work at jobs for adults. As with Riis, Hine's images helped change people's attitudes about what was acceptable, and that led to reforms. The two men are sometimes linked because of their efforts for reform. Both men are considered part of a tradition of photojournalism that focuses on social issues.

Hine photographed a child coal mine worker in 1908.

The two men's mutual respect blossomed into friendship in 1895, when Roosevelt became president of the New York Police Commission. The commission's job included fighting corruption on the city police force. By then, Riis was working for a different newspaper, the *Evening Sun*. He had become the best-known journalist in the city, thanks to his books. He also gave his magic lantern lectures across the country. After publishing *The Children of the*

Poor, Riis took fewer of his own photographs. As he had done before, he hired professional photographers to work for him. He also began to focus on public health problems. He documented pollution in New York's drinking water and wrote about the lives of rag pickers who sold unclean rags—a health hazard the city had outlawed.

Accompanied by Roosevelt, Riis set out to look for police corruption. Roosevelt knew that Riis had a long history of working with the police and could help uncover problems on the city's force. Riis had taken pictures of the conditions in the police stations housing the homeless. Riis, who had slept in the stations once himself, wanted the housing closed down. But first Roosevelt and Riis began taking late-night walks through New York City. They were trying to catch police officers who were not doing their jobs or were abusing their power and treating citizens unfairly.

They discovered that few police officers were walking the streets at night, as they were supposed to be. Some found hidden spots to take naps. Roosevelt and Riis also entered the tenements at night, to see the conditions while the residents slept. As a police commissioner, Roosevelt also sat on the city's Board of Health. Later, using evidence Riis provided, the board closed and then destroyed some of the worst tenements, places where crowded, dirty conditions had led to the deaths of many children.

Accompanied by Roosevelt, Riis set out to look for police corruption.

Police reformer Theodore Roosevelt was featured in an 1895 editorial cartoon in the *Washington Post*.

Riis also persuaded Roosevelt to shut down the police station housing. He told the commissioner about his own experience staying at a station 25 years before. Poor and homeless, Riis went to the station with a stray dog he had found. The officer in charge would not let Riis bring the dog in. Riis reluctantly left the dog outside in the rain and slept with "a foul and stewing crowd of tramps." During the night, one of them stole a gold locket from Riis, who told an officer. The policeman didn't believe him and called him a thief. Riis grew agitated, and the policeman kicked him out. At the doorway, Riis' dog attacked the officer leading him outside, and the man picked up the dog and smashed it against the stone steps, killing it.

That story had inflamed Riis' hatred of the police housing. After telling the tale to Roosevelt, the commissioner said, "I will smash them tomorrow." The city soon set up housing for the homeless that provided real beds and showers.

Roosevelt left the police commission in spring 1897, returning to Washington, D.C., to serve as assistant secretary of the Navy. A few months later, Riis watched with pride as New York City opened Mulberry Bend Park. It sat where some of the worst tenements had stood, until the Board of Health had them torn down. At the opening of the park, a city official said, "Without Riis, this park would not be here today."

Through the rest of the 1890s, Riis kept on reporting and working for reform. His photography, however, stopped in 1898. His last pictures were for an article about the destruction of an alley in Mulberry Bend. He retired as a journalist the following year so he could concentrate on his lectures. He also wrote several more books, including his autobiography, *The Making of an American.* Published in 1901, the book boosted Riis'

Riis captioned his photograph of a child in a dirty tenement hall *The Baby's Playground.*

fame across the country. By then Theodore Roosevelt had called Riis "New York's most useful citizen." In 1901, Roosevelt took office as vice president of the United States. Before the year was out, he became president, after William McKinley was killed by an assassin. When Roosevelt ran for president in 1904, Riis wrote a biography of him. As president, Roosevelt kept improving the lives of working Americans who sometimes struggled to survive. Riis, with his words and photos, had helped Roosevelt see the importance of reform.

ChapterFour
THE LASTING IMPACT OF JACOB RIIS

During the years of his friend Theodore Roosevelt's presidency from 1901 to 1909 and until his death in 1914, Jacob Riis kept spreading the message of reform. One of his last magazine articles was called "The Battle with the Slum." Its title was the same as that of his 1902 book. He also spoke at rallies across the country when Roosevelt unsuccessfully ran for president again in 1912. After Riis died, parks were named for him in New York and Chicago. Lillian Wald, another reformer who helped immigrants, praised Riis for "opening up the hearts of a people to emotion, and for the knowledge upon which to guide that emotion into constructive channels."

With his efforts, Riis showed the power of photography to bring the realities of urban life to the nation. He also demonstrated that, along with supplying facts, talking to the people affected by society's ills was a way to understand their lives. Other reformers would copy his methods as they tried to tackle poverty. And while he didn't think the government could solve all the problems, he saw the value of working with local officials to investigate them and then try to end them. Since his death, Riis' methods have been studied by students of sociology, history, photography, and journalism.

In a line that stretched out the door, homeless men and women waited to be allowed into the Mulberry Street police station to spend the night. The photo appeared in Riis' 1902 book, *The Battle With the Slum.*

Before he died, Riis gave his papers to the Library of Congress and the New York Public Library. He remained, in his own mind, a writer and not a photographer. His pictures were part of the larger works he did—his books and slide shows. People still respected the power of his images, but they were not widely seen for several decades after his death.

That finally changed in the 1940s, thanks to the efforts of Alexander Alland. A photographer, Alland read an article that compared his work to Riis' photographs. Alland had heard of Riis but wanted to know more about him, so he read *The Making of an American* and *How the Other Half Lives*. Alland discovered that Riis was more than a journalist and had taken some of the photos in his most famous book. Alland began to hunt for the negatives of Riis' photos. He contacted Riis' son Roger, who found 163 of his father's magic lantern slides. Alland began the slow process of converting the slides into film negatives so he could make prints. Then, in 1946, Roger Riis found a historical gold mine—more than 700 of his father's slides, glass negatives, and prints. Working with the Museum of the City of New York, Alland made prints of 50 of the best negatives.

The museum presented Alland's prints in May 1947 in a show called "The Battle With the Slum 1887–1897." The exhibit was displayed for more than six months, and it was highly praised. Beaumont Newhall, a photography historian, wrote in his book *The History of Photography* that the photos were "direct and penetrating, as raw as the sordid scenes which they so often represent." A photography magazine called the photos "one of the greatest sets of documentary pictures in American photographic history."

Slides of Riis' work, including an image of a lone man asleep on the floor of a police station, were later made into prints.

Newspapers, book publishers, and museums obtained clear copies of some of Riis' best photos (and the ones taken by his amateur helpers). A photography show at New York's Museum of Modern Art in 1949 included six of Riis' pictures, the most by any photographer represented in the exhibit. New York Mayor William O'Dwyer designated a week to honor Riis. The mayor praised him for helping the city and the rest of the country to gain "a newer and wider sense of civic conscience and responsibility."

Alland continued to work with Riis' images, and in 1974 his book *Jacob A. Riis: Photographer and Citizen* was published. It was partly a biography, but most of it featured 82 prints Alland had made from the restored negatives. The full-page pictures included Riis' first photograph, of the potter's field, as well as a cropped version of *Bandit's Roost* that emphasized the people lining the alley. One photo showed a peddler who was living in a flooded basement, which Riis had described in *The Children of the Poor*. The "Street Arabs" picture made the

Alland's work included a cropped version of *Bandit's Roost*, which Riis shot in one of New York's worst slums.

book too, along with Katie, the 9-year-old subject of the picture Riis called "I Scrubs."

Thanks to Alland's work, viewers could see more details than were visible in the 1890s. Garbage on the streets is clearer, ragged clothes and peeling plaster walls are sharper. The contrast between light and dark is stronger. Parts of a shadowy world come to life as Riis' flash goes off. As with the photo of Susie in *The Children of the Poor*, the images were sometimes blurred because the camera lens was not fast enough to capture subjects who were moving slightly. But that did not lessen their impact. If anything, those pictures showed that Riis had caught his subjects when they weren't expecting to be photographed, which made the photos more natural.

Ansel Adams, one of the best photographers of the 20th century, wrote the preface to Alland's book. He praised Alland's work in restoring the prints, noting how the people Riis photographed "live again for you in the print—as intensely as when their images were captured on the old dry plates of ninety years ago." Adams said part of the impact of the photos was that they placed the viewer in the scene. "[I]n viewing those prints," he wrote, "I find myself identified with the people photographed. I am walking in their alleys, standing in their rooms and sheds and workshops, looking in and out of their windows. And they in turn seem to be aware of me."

To mark the 100th anniversary of the publication of *How the Other Half Lives*, a *New York Times* photographer, Fred Conrad, was assigned in 1990 to take pictures like some made by Riis. Along with reporter Sam Roberts, Conrad visited tenements and talked with homeless people. They also went to Hart Island, where thousands of poor people were buried each year, just as they had been in Riis' day. Roberts noted in his story that Riis' work did lead to reform. Yet, as Conrad's pictures showed, the poor and tenements were still part of New York life. "At the turn of another century," Roberts wrote in 1991, "guns, drugs and race are redefining urban poverty, which seems to have grown deeper and more [widespread] since the time Riis prowled the streets of the Lower East Side as a police reporter." Roberts later helped make a documentary film called *The Other Half Revisited: The Legacy of Jacob A. Riis.*

As scholars looked at Riis and his influence, some pointed out that he was not the first person to photograph life in urban slums. At least two photographers in the United Kingdom had taken pictures of tenements there in the 1860s and 1870s. And Riis was not, as some people have claimed, the first photojournalist. Photojournalism puts its emphasis on the image, with perhaps only a few words in a caption to describe the scene. In 1900, Lawrence Veiller put together an exhibit that grouped

ALLAND HONORED JACOB RIIS

Alexander Alland photographed children playing in water from a fire hydrant.

Like Jacob Riis, Alexander Alland immigrated to the United States. Born in Russia in 1902, Alland arrived in New York City in 1923. He was a professional photographer, and in 1939 he took pictures for a book called *Portrait of New York*. Many of the photos showed various ethnic groups found in the city, which led a critic to compare Alland's work to Riis'. The two men also shared an interest in social reform. Their similarities led Alland to read several of Riis' books and then to hunt for his remaining photographs and negatives.

Never before, Alland wrote, had he "seen old photographs that could compare with the simple, powerful immediacy of those in his books." Restoring the negatives and making prints was hard. Riis had

not always used the proper chemicals to preserve the negatives, so some of the images had faded over time. Also, some images had areas that were too dark or too light. Alland later wrote, "I don't think he [Riis] was much concerned about technical perfection in his photographs." Alland also made some artistic changes, such as cropping some photos. Doing that made the central subject bigger and closer to the viewer.

Along with restoring Riis' photos and writing about him, Alland collected negatives and prints from other photographers and wrote a biography of Jessie Tarbox Beals, who was the first noted female photojournalist. Alland died in 1989, and some of his photos appeared in exhibits after his death.

Riis' photos with shots from other photographers. Veiller, according to photography historian Bonnie Yochelson, "used Riis's photographs in a manner that was as new to Riis as it was to the general public." Veiller let the photos, rather than words, show what tenement life was like. Yochelson also credits Lewis Hine with creating what would become photojournalism. But Yochelson appreciated Riis' historical importance. In 2015 she organized another exhibit of Riis' photos. Sam Roberts of *The New York Times* said the show "was a vivid reminder of the camera's power and unique perspective." Daniel Czitrom, a history professor who co-wrote a book about Riis with Yochelson, said, "Today, no one really reads Riis anymore, and yet the photographs remain incredibly moving."

Perhaps that's one reason Riis' images of the slums still command attention. Immigration issues still stir strong debate. Poverty remains a central problem for U.S. cities. And distrust or fear of people of different religious or ethnic backgrounds is also a concern. Riis' images capture what life was like at a time when few people were documenting "the other half." They are important as history, but also as reminders that the challenges of ending poverty and promoting acceptance remain.

Riis' photos revealed the dreadful circumstances of New York City's poor and led to major reforms. After he showed the horrors of living in the Gotham Court tenement (above), it was torn down.

Timeline

1849

Jacob Riis is born May 3 in Ribe, Denmark

1870

Riis arrives in New York City

1873

Riis begins working as a reporter for the New York News Association

1884

New York's Tenement House Commission issues a report about the worsening conditions in the slums

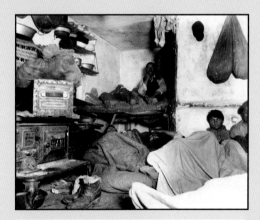

1887

Working with several amateur photographers, Riis takes his first pictures of tenement life in New York

1875

Riis buys a newspaper in Brooklyn

1877

The *New York Tribune* hires Riis as a reporter and soon assigns him to cover police news

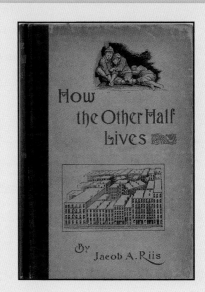

1888

Riis buys his first camera; he gives magic lantern shows that feature his photographs

1890

Riis' book *How the Other Half Lives: Studies Among the Tenements of New York* is published

Timeline

1892

Riis' book *The Children of the Poor* is published

1895

Theodore Roosevelt becomes a police commissioner in New York and asks Riis to help him look for police corruption

1898

Riis takes his last photographs, though he continues to write and give lectures

1946

Roger Riis, Jacob Riis' son, discovers hundreds of his father's slides and negatives and gives them to photographer Alexander Alland

1947

After Alland restores 50 of Riis' photos, the Museum of the City of New York puts them on display, and Riis begins to receive credit for his photography

1901

Riis' autobiography, *The Making of an American*, is published

1914

Riis dies May 26; he was 65

1974

Alland's book, *Jacob A. Riis: Photographer and Citizen*, which features 82 of Riis' restored photos, is published

2015

The Museum of the City of New York hosts another major exhibit of Riis' work

1991

The New York Times publishes a story that features photos similar to Riis' images and shows the lasting presence of poverty in the city

Glossary

composition—the way the subjects in photos are arranged and how light strikes them

corruption—willingness to do things that are wrong or illegal to get money, favors, or power

cropping—cutting away part of a photo to improve framing or to focus on one part of it

discrimination—unfair treatment of a person or group, often because of race, religion, gender, sexual preference, or age

indictment—accusation of wrongdoing

muckrake—to search out and publicly expose misconduct of a prominent person or business

nativists—people born in the United States who favor a policy of protecting their interests over those of immigrants; nativists want to restrict immigration by race and national origin

negatives—reversed photographic images; prints can be made from negatives

photojournalist—photographer who takes photos of news events

realism—representing a person or thing in a way that is true to life

squalid—very dirty and miserable, especially as a result of poverty or neglect

stereotypical—based on overly simplified or untrue ideas about a person or group

tenement—rundown apartment building, especially one that is crowded and in a poor part of a city

Additional Resources

Further Reading

Berne, Emma Carlson. *The Presidency of Theodore Roosevelt: Leading from the Bully Pulpit.* North Mankato, Minn.: Compass Point Books, 2015.

Bliss, John. *Nineteenth-century Migration to America.* Chicago: Raintree, 2012.

Burgan, Michael. *Breaker Boys: How a Photograph Helped End Child Labor.* Mankato, Minn.: Compass Point Books, 2012.

McNeese, Tim. *The Gilded Age and Progressivism, 1891–1913.* New York: Chelsea House, 2010.

Critical Thinking Questions

What experiences in Jacob Riis' childhood and immigrant experience shaped his concern for the poor of New York City? Use examples from the text.

Why was the improved flash technology so important for Riis' photography? How did it help him in his work?

How did Riis' work relate to what the Progressives were trying to do across the United States? Do you see parallels in what is happening in the United States today? Why or why not?

Internet Sites

Use FactHound to find Internet sites related to this book.
Visit *www.facthound.com*
Just type in 9780756556181 and go.

Source Notes

Page 4, line 9: Jacob A. Riis, *The Making of an American*. New York: The MacMillan Company, 1901, p. 203. https://ia802205.us.archive.org/2/items/makingofamerican00riisrich/makingofamerican00riisrich_bw.pdf

Page 6, line 1: Ibid., p. 267.

Page 6, line 26: Ibid., p. 268.

Page 7, line 11: Bonnie Yochelson and Daniel Czitrom. *Rediscovering Jacob Riis: Exposure Journalism and Photography in Turn-of-the-Century New York*. Chicago: The University of Chicago Press, 2014, p. 142.

Page 9, line 3: *The Making of an American*, p. 274.

Page 11, line 4: Ibid., p. 271.

Page 12, line 2: Tom Buk-Swienty. *The Other Half: The Life of Jacob Riis and the World of Immigrant America*, trans. Annette Buk-Swienty. New York: W.W. Norton and Co., 2008, p.197.

Page 12, line 19: Ibid., p. 215.

Page 12, line 23: Ibid.

Page 15, caption: Jacob A. Riis. *How the Other Half Lives: Studies Among the Tenements of New York*. New York: Charles Scribner's Sons, 1890, p. 200. https://books.google.com/books?id=zhcv_oA5dwgC&printsec=frontcover&source=gbs_ge_mary_r&cad=0#v=onepage&q=fix%20it&f=false

Page 17, line 3: *The Making of an American*, p. 8.

Page 18, line 17: Ibid., p. 38.

Page 21, line 24: *The Other Half: The Life of Jacob Riis and the World of Immigrant America*, p. 103.

Page 22, line 16: *The Making of an American*, p. 184.

Page 22, line 26: Ibid., p. 188.

Page 25, line 3: Ibid., p. 206

Page 25, line 6: Ibid., p. 223.

Page 27, line 20: Thomas Bailey Aldrich. "Unguarded Gates." *The Atlantic Monthly*, Vol. 0070, Issue 417, p. 57. July 1892. 15 Dec. 2016. http://ebooks.library.cornell.edu/cgi/t/text/pageviewer-idx?c=atla;cc=atla;rgn=full%20text;idno=atla0070-1;didno=atla0070-1;view=image;seq=0063;node=atla0070-1%3A6

Page 28, line 6: *How the Other Half Lives: Studies Among the Tenements of New York*, p. 18.

Page 29, caption: Riis, Jacob A. *The Battle With the Slum*. New York: Macmillan & Co., 1902, p. 46. https://archive.org/details/ldpd_6697366_000

Page 30, line 7: *Rediscovering Jacob Riis: Exposure Journalism and Photography in Turn-of-the-Century New York*, p. 61.

Page 30, line 18: *The Making of an American*, p. 271.

Page 31, line 4: Ibid., p. 265.

Page 31, line 6: Ibid.

Page 33, line 2: *How the Other Half Lives*, p. 197.

Page 33, line 19: *Rediscovering Jacob Riis*, p. 105.

Page 33, line 22: *The Making of an American*, pp. 213-214.

Page 34, line 9: *The Other Half: The Life of Jacob Riis and the World of Immigrant America*, p. 28.

Page 35, line 6: *The Making of an American*, p. 287-288.

Page 36, line 7: Ibid., p. 290.

Page 36, line 18: Jacob A. Riis. *The Children of the Poor*. New York: Charles Scribner's Sons, 1908, p. v. https://ia801408.us.archive.org/33/items/childrenofpoor00riisuoft/childrenofpoor00riisuoft.pdf

Page 37, line 6: Ibid., p. 60.

Page 37, line 12: Ibid., p. 61.

Page 38, line 2: Ibid.

Page 38, line 26: Ibid., pp. 40–41.

Page 39, line 7: Ibid., p. 4.

Page 40, line 3: Ibid., p. 8.

Page 40, line 20: Jacob A. Riis. *Theodore Roosevelt, The Citizen*. Washington, D.C.: Johnson, Wynne Company, 1904, p. 131.

Page 40, line 22: Theodore Roosevelt. Stephen Brennan, ed. *An Autobiography of Theodore Roosevelt*. New York: Skyhorse Pub., 2011, p. 158.

Page 43, line 8: *The Making of an American*, p. 71.

Page 44, line 10: Alexander Alland Sr. *Jacob A. Riis: Photographer & Citizen*. Millerton, N.Y.: Aperture, 1974, p. 33.

Page 44, line 19: *The Other Half: The Life of Jacob Riis and the World of Immigrant America*, p. 255.

Page 45, line 2: Ibid., p. 273.

Page 46, line 11: "Jacob Riis: Revealing 'How the Other Half Lives.'" Library of Congress Exhibition. 14 April–5 Sept. 2016. 16 Feb. 2017. http://www.loc.gov/exhibits/jacob-riis/legacy.html#obj108

Page 48, line 25: Beaumont Newhall. *The History of Photography from 1839 to the Present Day*. New York: Museum of Modern Art, 1949, p. 170

Page 48, line 28: *Jacob A. Riis: Photographer & Citizen*, p. 46.

Page 49, line 9: Ibid., p. 48.

Page 51, line 19: Ibid., p. 6.

Page 51, line 23: Ibid.

Page 52, line 12: Sam Roberts. "New York in the Nineties." *The New York Times*. 29 Sept. 1991. 14 Dec. 2016. http://www.nytimes.com/1991/09/29/magazine/new-york-in-the-nineties.html

Page 53, col. 1, line 11: *Jacob A. Riis: Photographer & Citizen*, p. 43.

Page 53, col. 2, line 4: Ibid., p. 45.

Page 54, line 3: *Rediscovering Jacob Riis*, p. 223.

Page 54, line 11: Sam Roberts. "Revealing Riis's Other Half of New York." *The New York Times*. 22 Oct. 2015. 14 Dec. 2016. http://lens.blogs.nytimes.com/2015/10/22/revealing-riiss-other-half-of-new-york/?_r=0.

Page 54, line 14: Sewell Chan. "Revisting the Other Half of Jacob Riis." *The New York Times*. 28 Feb. 2008. 15 Feb. 2017. https://cityroom.blogs.nytimes.com/2008/02/28/revisiting-the-other-half-of-jacob-riis/

Select Bibliography

Aldrich, Thomas Bailey. "Unguarded Gates." *The Atlantic Monthly*, Vol. 0070, Issue 417, p. 57. July 1892. 15 Dec. 2016. http://ebooks.library.cornell.edu/cgi/t/text/pageviewer-idx?c=atla;cc=atla;rgn=full%20text;idno=atla0070-1;didno=atla0070-1;view=image;seq=0063;node=atla0070-1%3A6

Alland, Alexander, Sr. *Jacob A. Riis: Photographer & Citizen.* Millerton, N.Y.: Aperture, 1974.

Buk-Swienty, Tom. *The Other Half: The Life of Jacob Riis and the World of Immigrant America*, trans. Annette Buk-Swienty. New York: W.W. Norton and Co., 2008.

Chan, Sewell. "Revisting the Other Half of Jacob Riis." *The New York Times.* 28 Feb. 2008. 15 Feb. 2017. https://cityroom.blogs.nytimes.com/2008/02/28/revisiting-the-other-half-of-jacob-riis

Constitutional Rights Foundation. "History Lesson 2: History of Immigration From the 1850s to the Present." Educating About Immigration. 15 Dec. 2016. http://crfimmigrationed.org/index.php/lessons-for-teachers/72-history-lesson-2

Daniels, Roger. *Coming to America: A History of Immigration and Ethnicity in American Life.* New York: Perennial, 2002.

Davis, Kay. "Documenting 'The Other Half': The Social Reform Photography of Jacob Riis & Lewis Hine. Digital Humanities Projects. The University of Virginia. 15 Dec. 2016. http://xroads.virginia.edu/~ma01/davis/photography/home/home.html

De Forest, Robert W., and Lawrence Veiller, eds. *The Tenement House Problem: Including the Report of the New York State Tenement House Commission of 1900.* Vol. 1. New York: The Macmillan Company, 1903. https://books.google.com/books?id=3IMgAQAAMAAJ&dq=1884+tenement+house+commission&source=gbs_navlinks_s

"Guide to the Alexander Alland Photograph Collection 1885–1905, 1940." New-York Historical Society Museum & Library. 15 Dec. 2016. http://dlib.nyu.edu/findingaids/html/nyhs/alland/bioghist.html

Gup, Ted. "The 1890 Book I Had to Have." *The New York Times.* 11 Jan. 2014. 14 Feb. 2017. https://opinionator.blogs.nytimes.com/2014/01/11/the-1890-book-i-had-to-have/?ref=opinion&_r=1

Harding, Colin. "Victorians Poked Fun At The First Instantaneous, Hidden Cameras." National Media Museum. 12 Sept. 2013. 15 Dec. 2016. http://blog.nationalmediamuseum.org.uk/detective-camera-stirns-waistcoat-camera/

"An Introduction to Lantern History." The Magic Lantern Society. 15 Dec. 2016. http://www.magiclantern.org.uk/history/history01.php

"Jacob Riis: Revealing 'How the Other Half Lives.'" Library of Congress Exhibition. 14 April–5 Sept. 2016. 15 Feb. 2017. http://www.loc.gov/exhibits/jacob-riis/index.html

"Jacob Riis: Shedding Light On NYC's 'Other Half.'" *All Things Considered.* NPR. 30 June 2008. 15 Feb. 2017. http://www.npr.org/templates/story/story.php?storyId=91981589

"Making Sense of Photos: Who Took the Photograph?" History Matters. 15 Dec. 2016. http://historymatters.gmu.edu/mse/photos/question1.html

Mastropolo, Frank. "How Bandit's Roost Blossomed Into Chinatown's Columbus Park." *Bedford & Bowery.* 10 April 2015. 15 Dec. 2016. http://bedfordandbowery.com/2015/04/how-bandits-roost-blossomed-into-chinatowns-columbus-park/

Morris, Edmund. *The Rise of Theodore Roosevelt.* New York: Modern Library, 2001.

Newhall, Beaumont. *The History of Photography from 1839 to the Present Day.* New York: Museum of Modern Art, 1949.

Riis, Jacob A. *The Battle With the Slum.* New York: Macmillan & Co., 1902. https://archive.org/details/ldpd_6697366_000

Riis, Jacob A. *The Children of the Poor.* New York: Charles Scribner's Sons, 1908. https://ia801408.us.archive.org/33/items/childrenofpoor00riisuoft/childrenofpoor00riisuoft.pdf

Riis, Jacob A. "How the Other Half Lives: Studies Among the Tenements." *Scribner's Magazine*, Vol. VI, No. 6, December 1889, pp. 643–662. 16 Dec. 2016. http://www.unz.org/Pub/Scribners-1889dec-00643?View=PDF

Riis, Jacob A. *How the Other Half Lives: Studies Among the Tenements of New York.* New York: Charles Scribner's Sons, 1890. https://books.google.com/books?id=zhcv_oA5dwgC&printsec=frontcover&source=gbs_ge_summary_r&cad=0#v=onepage&q&f=false

Riis, Jacob A. *The Making of an American.* New York: The MacMillan Company, 1901.

Riis, Jacob A. *Theodore Roosevelt, The Citizen.* Washington, D.C.: Johnson, Wynne Company, 1904. https://books.google.com/books?id=CDNEAQAAMAAJ&pg=PR16&dq=roosevelt+%22i+will+smash+them+tomorrow%22&hl=en&sa=X&ved=0ahUKEwiypZC_udPQAhXl5oMKHfRQAbIQ6AEIHTAA#v=onepage&q=roosevelt%20%22i%20will%20smash%20them%20tomorrow%22&f=false

Roberts, Sam. "New York in the Nineties." *The New York Times.* 29 Sept. 1991. 14 Dec. 2016. http://www.nytimes.com/1991/09/29/magazine/new-york-in-the-nineties.html

Roberts, Sam. "Revealing Riis's Other Half of New York." *The New York Times.* 22 Oct. 2015. 14 Dec. 2016. http://lens.blogs.nytimes.com/2015/10/22/revealing-riiss-other-half-of-new-york/?_r=0

Roosevelt, Theodore. Stephen Brennan, ed. *An Autobiography of Theodore Roosevelt.* New York: Skyhorse Pub., 2011.

Smith, Terry. Book Reviews: *Reading American Photographs: Images as History, Mathew Brady to Walker Evans.* Alan Trachtenberg; *Symbols of Ideal Life: Social Documentary Photography in America 1890–1950.* Maren Stange; *Documenting America, 1935–1943.* Carl Fleischhauer, Beverly W. Brannan. *Archives of American Art Journal*, Vol. 31, No. 2, 1991, pp. 21–31.

Yochelson, Bonnie. *Jacob Riis.* New York: Phaidon, 2001.

Yochelson, Bonnie, and Daniel Czitrom. *Rediscovering Jacob Riis: Exposure Journalism and Photography in Turn-of-the-Century New York.* Chicago: The University of Chicago Press, 2014.

Index

About the Author
Michael Burgan has written many books for children and young adults during his 20 years as a freelance writer. Most of his books have focused on history. Burgan has won several awards for his writing. He lives in Santa Fe, New Mexico.